Sports and My Body

Gymnastics

Catherine Veitch

Heinemann Library
Chicago, Illinois

www.heinemannraintree.com
Visit our website to find out
more information about
Heinemann-Raintree books.

To order:

☎ Phone 888-454-2279

💻 Visit www.heinemannraintree.com
to browse our catalog and order online.

© 2009 Raintree
an imprint of Capstone Global Library, LLC
Chicago, Illinois

Customer Service: 888-454-2279

Visit our website at www.heinemannraintree.com

Edited by Siân Smith, Rebecca Rissman, and
Charlotte Guillain
Designed by Joanna Hinton-Malivoire
Picture research by Ruth Blair
Production by Duncan Gilbert

Originated by Chroma Graphics (Overseas) Pte. Ltd
Printed and bound in China by South China Printing
Company Ltd

13 12 11 10
10 9 8 7 6 5 4 3 2

Library of Congress Cataloging-in-Publication
Veitch, Catherine.
  Gymnastics / Catherine Veitch.
    p. cm. -- (Sports and my body)
  Includes bibliographical references and index.
  ISBN 978-1-4329-3454-5 (hc) -- ISBN 978-1-4329-
3459-0 (pb) 1. Gymnastics--Juvenile literature. I. Title.
  GV461.3.V54 2008
  796.44--dc22
                              2009007084

Acknowledgments
The author and publishers are grateful to the following
for permission to reproduce copyright material:
© Capstone Global Library Ltd p. 22 (Trevor Clifford);
Corbis pp. 7 (Strauss/Curtis), 9 (Kevin Dodge), 10
(Anna Peisl/zefa), 12 (image100), 14 (Fancy/Veer),
16 (Adriane Moll/zefa), 23 (Kevin Dodge); Getty
Images pp. 4 (Alistair Berg), 5, 23 (Clive Brunskill), 6,
23 (Frederick J. Brown/AFP), 13 (Susanna Price/DK),
17 (J. Clarke), 19 (Ableimages/Riser), 20 (Victoria
Blackie/Photographer's Choice); Photolibrary pp. 8, 23
(GoGo Images), 15, 23 (Westend61), 18 (Big Cheese);
Shutterstock pp. 11 (© Jiang Dao Hua), 21 (© Monkey
Business Images).

Cover photograph of girls doing floor exercises
reproduced with permission of Corbis/Anna Peisl/zefa.
Back cover images reproduced with permission of
Corbis: 1. child stretching (© Kevin Dodge); 2. child in a
gym, bending backwards (© image100).

Every effort has been made to contact copyright holders
of material reproduced in this book. Any omissions will
be rectified in subsequent printings if notice is given to
the publishers.

Disclaimer
All the Internet addresses (URLs) given in this book were
valid at the time of going to press. However, due to the
dynamic nature of the Internet, some addresses may
have changed, or sites may have changed or ceased to
exist since publication. While the author and publishers
regret any inconvenience this may cause readers, no
responsibility for any such changes can be accepted by
either the author or the publishers.

Contents

Some words are shown in bold, **like this**. You can find them in the glossary on page 23.

What Is Gymnastics?

Gymnastics is a type of exercise.
You can do jumps, rolls, and **balance skills** in gymnastics.

You can do gymnastics on the floor or on an **apparatus**, such as the rings.

How Do I Learn Gymnastics?

You need an adult to teach you gymnastics. A teacher at your school or a gymnastics **coach** could teach you in a gym.

You need to be strong to do gymnastics. At first a teacher may help you learn to **balance**.

How Do I Use My Arms and Hands?

You use your arms to swing under a bar. You use your hands to grip the bar tightly so you do not fall off.

You can stretch out your arms to help you **balance** on a beam. You can also make different shapes with your hands and arms.

How Do I Use My Legs and Feet?

You use your legs to do the splits. You should stretch your legs and point your toes in the splits.

You use your legs when you land after a jump. You should bend your knees when you land.

How Do I Use the Rest of My Body?

You can bend your back to make a bridge. This makes an arch shape with your body.

You can tuck yourself into a ball and roll backward or forward on a mat.

What other ways can you roll?

What Happens to My Body When I Do Gymnastics?

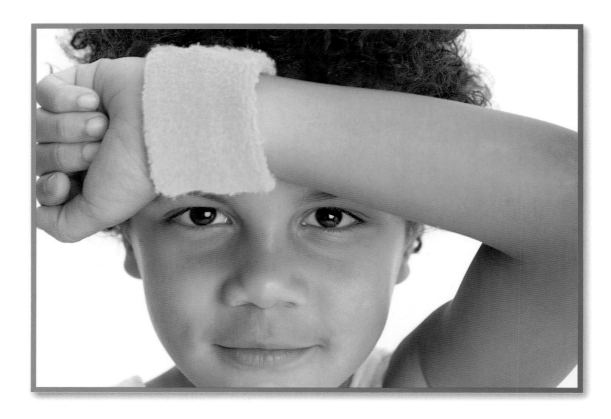

When you do gymnastics you will start to feel warm and sweaty. You will also feel out of breath.

muscle

Your heart will beat faster. The **muscles** in your arms and legs might ache and feel tired.

How Does It Feel to Do Gymnastics?

Gymnastics is a good way to have fun. You might make new friends as you do gymnastics together.

It feels good to get better at gymnastics. As you get stronger you can learn more **skills**.

How Do I Stay Safe Doing Gymnastics?

You should always warm up before you do gymnastics. Stretching your **muscles** warms them up and keeps you from getting hurt.

It is important to listen to your **coach**.
When you use an **apparatus**, make
sure nobody is in the way. Also, make
sure you always use safety mats.

Does Gymnastics Make Me Healthy?

Gymnastics is good exercise and will help you keep fit. You should also eat healthy food and drink plenty of water.

To stay healthy you need to get plenty of rest, too. Then you can have fun getting lots of other kinds of exercise.

Gymnastics Equipment

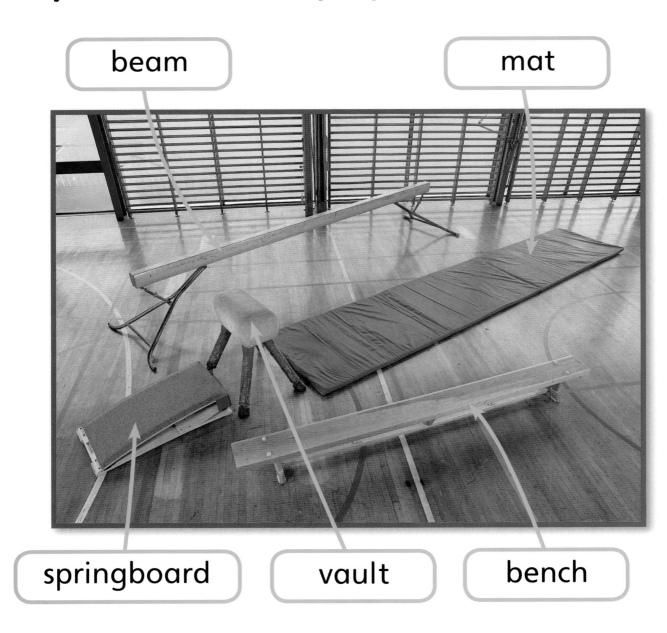

beam

mat

springboard

vault

bench

Glossary

 **apparatus** equipment. People often use large apparatuses in gymnastics, such as beams to balance on. See page 22 for examples of different apparatuses.

 **balance** keep yourself or an object steady so that it does not fall

 **coach** trainer. A coach helps people to learn and become better at something.

 **muscle** part of your body that helps you to move. Exercise can make muscles bigger and stronger.

 **skill** ability to do something well. You can develop different skills through training and practice.

Index

Find Out More

www.thespringboard.org.uk
Find out about children who do gymnastics and learn more about the sport.

http://kids.nationalgeographic.com/Games/ActionGames/Geogames-monkey-bars-gymnastics
Play the Monkey Bar game to learn about gymnastics!